Worms
Help Soil

SRA

Columbus, OH

SRAonline.com

 SRA

Send all inquiries to this address:
SRA/McGraw-Hill
4400 Easton Commons
Columbus, OH 43219

ISBN: 978-0-07-608527-9
MHID: 0-07-608527-9

1 2 3 4 5 6 7 8 9 NOR 13 12 11 10 09 08 07

This is more than dirt. A woman is holding good, dark soil. How does the soil get this way?

This is an earthworm. When it rains its
home fills with water. It comes out of the ground
for air.

Earthworms help the soil. They make tunnels.
See the tiny hairs on their bodies? They help the
worms move fast.

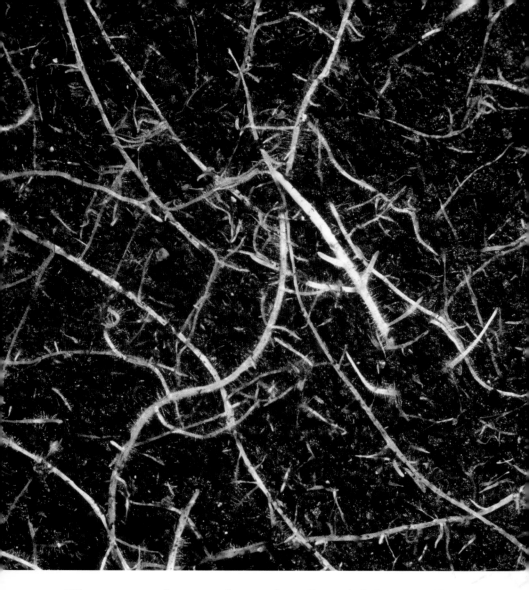

The worms' tunnels make the soil loose. The soil gets oxygen, and water can pass through. Too much water can kill plant roots.

Earthworms are not fussy eaters. They eat leaves and stems. Earthworms even eat soil. They put everything they eat back into the soil.

Worms make castings. Castings have nutrients and minerals. Castings feel soft. Plants use the nutrients right away.

You can make good soil. In the fall start a worm pile. Gather grass, leaves, and vegetable peels. Make the pile two feet high.

Cover the pile with dirt, and wait for the earthworms to invade. If a plant sprouts in your pile, let it grow.

In the spring your soil will be ready. Take soil from the center and feed it to your plants. Then thank the earthworms!

Vocabulary

tunnels (tun´ əlz) (page 5) *n.* Plural form of **tunnel:** An underground passageway.

fussy (fus´ ē) (page 7) *adj.* Hard to please.

stems (stemz) (page 7) *n.* Plural form of **stem:** The main part of a plant.

minerals (min´ ər əlz) (page 8) *n.* Plural form of **mineral:** Something found underground and used as food for plants growing in soil.

invade (in vād´) (page 10) *v.* To enter without an invitation.

sprouts (sprouts) (page 10) *v.* Begins to grow.

Comprehension Focus:
Cause and Effect

1. Reread page 6. What may happen to the roots with too much water?

2. If you make a worm pile in the fall, what will happen?